Dolphins at Grassy Key

Marcia Seligson   Photographs by George Ancona

Macmillan Publishing Company   New York   Collier Macmillan Publishers   London

The author wishes to express her appreciation to Jayne and Mandy Rodriguez and the staff of the Dolphin Research Center for all their support, and to offer special thanks to Jayne Rodriguez for her astute editing of the manuscript. And for her review of the manuscript, the author also thanks Martha Hiatt of the New York Aquarium.

Design by George Ancona

To Tom,

with love

—M.S.

To Marina,

our very own

sea sprite

— G.A.

There is a place in Grassy Key, Florida, on the Gulf of Mexico, called the Dolphin Research Center. The center is a unique spot, the only privately owned dolphin research facility of its kind in North America. Sixteen dolphins live there, not in tanks but in large, penned-in areas of the Gulf. They range in age from infants to senior citizens. Through the years the center's work has included training dolphins to perform in aquariums and movies, researching dolphin language and communication, and treating at the Dolphin Critical Care Unit overstressed or ill dolphins sent from aquariums all over the world.

One of the regular duties of the staff of seventeen is to take visitors on a variety of educational journeys through the center. Among these is a one-hour tour in which visitors observe the feeding, training, and care of the dolphins. The most unforgettable, thrilling part of the tour comes during the last minutes, when visitors are invited to swim and frolic with the giant dolphins, grab on to their dorsal fins while being pulled rapidly through the water, or give them a signal and watch them leap high into the air right over the visitors' bodies!

For visitors who wish to participate in, rather than observe, the feeding, training, and care of the dolphins, the center offers a program called Dolphinlab. Visitors taking part in Dolphinlab live near the Dolphin Research Center for two to seven days and share in the staff's work from morning until night. In the evenings they attend staff-taught classes on dolphins and other marine life, and on the geography of Florida. Of course, they also swim with the dolphins and just spend quiet time on the docks, playing with their favorites.

The Dolphin Research Center was started about thirty years ago. It is now owned by Mandy and Jayne Rodriguez, who live there with their children, Shannon, Shawn, and baby Kelly Jayne. Mandy and Jayne met while working at the New England Aquarium in Boston (she was the first sea lion trainer there). They both have extensive knowledge of dolphins and a deep love for these creatures, which is also true of the whole staff.

The center is one of the few facilities in North America that keeps the dolphins in a natural seawater environment, resulting in an excellent record of health, long life, and successful reproduction among them. It is small, homey, informal, and completely dedicated to the welfare of the dolphins. It is the only such place whose primary goal is to educate the public about the remarkable dolphin.

Dolphins are mammals, first cousins of pilot whales, killer whales, and porpoises. The most familiar of the thirty-eight species of dolphins are the Atlantic bottlenose dolphins—the ones that appear to have a big, broad grin on their faces. All the dolphins at the center, except one, are of the bottlenose variety, since these swim closer to shore and can be captured and maintained more easily than other, deep-water species.

The bottlenose dolphins weigh six hundred to seven hundred pounds and can swim more than twenty-five miles per hour in short spurts. Although females can live equally long in either situation, the lifespan of the male might be thirty to forty years in captivity, but only twenty in the wild. These dolphins have no sense of smell, but they have good vision and sense of taste, and are very sensitive to touch (their skin feels like wet rubber, and they love being stroked by the students and trainers).

But the dolphins' most powerful sense is an amazing built-in sonar system of detection. They can locate and identify objects in their path by sending out high-frequency sound waves that bounce off an object and produce an echo. This system, called "echolocation," is believed to be sharper and more accurate than our eyes and ears working together. And it is believed by many to be a means of communication among dolphins. A dolphin can perceive sounds ten times higher in pitch than can a human.

The brains of dolphins are 20 percent bigger than ours, and dolphins have been on earth 65 million years longer, their brains evolving the entire time. That is one reason some scientists think dolphins may be the most advanced creatures on earth. Scientists hope that by discovering how dolphins communicate, one day we may be able to share a language with them and cross the bridge that separates humans from animals.

Another theory about dolphin intelligence is that because they have to breathe voluntarily—not automatically, without thought, as we do—they have to be doing some kind of "thinking" all the time. Since dolphins can't sleep fully or they would stop breathing, we believe that one half of the brain sleeps while the other is awake. We also measure dolphins' intelligence by their great capacity to imitate other creatures, by the speed with which they learn and solve problems, and by their reaction to communication from people and from one another.

Dolphins are curious and quick to learn, which is why they are trained to perform in shows. It is also the reason the military trains them to search for hidden explosives in the ocean. They are extremely protective of one another and will encircle injured pals, raise them to the surface, and hold them there while they breathe. And they have been known to push shipwrecked people to shore, protecting them from circling sharks.

Dolphins seem to have a natural desire to perform. Even in the open ocean, sailors report that dolphins following their boats will execute spontaneous leaps and backflips. And they appear to be genuinely attracted to people. In an aquarium that was shut down temporarily, the dolphins that were accustomed to performing for large audiences several times each day became ill with stomach problems when their performances were canceled. When the shows started again, the dolphins quickly became healthy and lively.

If they wished, the dolphins at the Dolphin Research Center could easily escape by going under or over the plastic fences. But they never do. Once, a sick dolphin got out, and several others leaped over the fence, found her, and escorted her home. Sometimes the dolphins break out by pushing their snouts into the fences, but after a few hours of frolicking in the open sea, they always return.

A typical morning at the Dolphin Research Center begins with feeding at 9:00 A.M. Ten thousand pounds of herring and capelin are used every month, or three hundred to four hundred pounds a day. The fish is trucked in from Canada, New England, and Newfoundland.

The staff is very fussy about the fish fed to the dolphins and will throw out fish whose flesh is open or whose skin is broken. From each fish delivery, they send a sample to a lab to measure its calories and fat content. And to prevent bacteria from growing, they thaw the frozen fish in the refrigerator over the twenty-four-hour period before feeding.

Since the dolphins don't drink much seawater, food is even more important to them than to most water creatures. They get the water they need mainly from the moisture content of the fish they eat. If they don't feel well and stop eating for a few days, the staff has to put water into them by tube so that they don't become dehydrated.

The dolphins are each fed between ten and twenty-six pounds of food a day. The morning feeding is light, so that the dolphins can be active during the day. The feeding at 4:00 P.M. is heavier.

Twice a week the staff feeds all the dolphins vitamins. They insert these into the gills of the fish the dolphins eat, and give a double dose to pregnant or nursing dolphins. Each dolphin has its own color-coded food pail, since each one gets a different amount of food and since a sick dolphin will have medicine put into its food. The staff keeps accurate records of which dolphin eats what.

The fish house is always spotless. Whenever they can, Shannon and Shawn help the staff scrub down the food pails, the walls, and the floor, which is done daily.

Sometimes visitors are allowed to feed the dolphins. When the dolphins see and "hear" the fish, they all circle around the dock. As visitors call their names, saying, "This is for you, Merina," or "Come here, Captiva," the dolphins swim up and open their huge snouts, with eighty-eight razor-sharp teeth apiece. The visitors then lay three or four fish at a time in each dolphin's mouth. The hungry dolphins are surprisingly gentle, never once snapping at the visitors' fingers.

Like people, dolphins are unique, with distinct personalities. And a lot of the dolphins' behavior is comic and naughty, or silly and affectionate.

Tursi, for instance, has a missing left eye, and if she doesn't feel like performing, she will turn her blind eye to the trainer, pretending that she can't see the commands. But in many of the training sessions, she is among the most creative, improvising as well as responding to commands.

Eleven-year-old Nat has the most patience, so the staff does the most research with him. He is the only male who is allowed by the mother dolphins to baby-sit their offspring. Nat understands fifteen word commands, which is quite an accomplishment, since most dolphins respond only to hand signals.

Afro came from Baltimore's National Aquarium with bleeding ulcers from stress. She is completely healed, and she is madly in love with the dolphin Joe, who once broke through the fence separating them. Joe is being trained for release into the open waters.

Theresa and Rosie are flirts who prefer kissing male humans to female humans. Once, when the trainer asked Theresa to kiss a man's wife, she spit water in the woman's face and went right back to offering her affection to the man.

Little Bit, the oldest resident, used to tip over boats with kids in them as a prank. She loves children and follows them like a magnet whenever they are on the dock or in the water. She became both a mother *and* a grandmother in 1988.

A big part of every day is the session in which the trainers work with the dolphins. No session lasts more than forty-five minutes, because the dolphins get bored easily and just swim away. Dolphins don't do "tricks," the trainers say. Tricks are make-believe illusions, or sleights of hand, done by magicians. Dolphins perform "behaviors," which they learn. Sometimes it takes dolphins two years to learn a behavior such as the tail walk, because their bodies have to become strong enough. But since it is natural to them, dolphins can learn the high dive in only two weeks. Just one trainer will teach a dolphin a particular behavior, so that the dolphin will not be confused while learning.

The dolphins usually don't respond to words, although Nat knows "tummy" and will roll over when the trainer shouts the word. And when the trainer yells "Rock," he will disappear to the bottom of the sea and return with a rock in his mouth.

All the dolphins love to tease people who are watching them by making different sounds—squawks, squeaks, clicks—or by flipping over and soaking the people on the dock. Delphi once performed in an aquarium and learned to do a belly-flop dive just by mimicking the clowns. When he came to the Dolphin Research Center, he taught his pals the same behavior, and now they like to show off for the human audience.

The trainers at the center have from one to twenty years' experience, and they show great enthusiasm and affection for the dolphins, whether or not the dolphins do something right. If the dolphins *do* respond the way the trainers want them to, the trainers give them not only affection but also extravagant praise and, of course, food. And because the dolphins become restless quickly, the trainers often leap around like cheerleaders. After all, if the dolphins are bored, they will stop taking commands.

Since dolphins can be jealous of one another, the
trainers have to be careful not to pay more attention to
one than to the others. When Linda, a trainer, is working
with Captiva, the other dolphins do dives and tail walks
without being signaled, so that she will notice them, too.

The trained dolphins respond immediately to their trainers. When Della, another trainer, points at a dolphin, meaning "Stay here and watch me for a further signal," the dolphin stays. When she signals a high dive, circling her arms over her head twice and shouting "Dive," the results are spectacular!

But the dolphins don't respond to every single human. They have to learn to trust people individually. The trainers win their trust by hugging and kissing them all the time. And when strangers visit, the trainers have to promise the dolphins that the visitors are okay.

Visitors are taught some of the basic signals and are invited to use them on the dolphins. When the visitors make mistakes, the dolphins look as though they are laughing at the visitors. Then the dolphins do exactly as they please.

One of the most popular behaviors with visitors is the one in which the dolphin stands up in the water and offers a fin for a handshake. It takes a couple of months to train dolphins to do this, mostly because their stomach muscles have to become very strong for them to stand erect.

In order to teach this behavior, the trainer needs three tools: a whistle, a bucket of fish, and a target (a long stick with a ball on the end). First the trainer puts the target in the water. When the curious dolphin approaches, she blows her whistle and throws it a fish. She repeats this several times. Whenever the dolphin gets close to the target, she blows the whistle and throws a fish. The dolphin learns to associate the whistle with the reward. As the dolphin touches the target, the trainer lifts it higher out of the water. Gradually the dolphin learns that the goal is to touch the target with its snout. Soon the trainer touches the dolphin's snout with her hand, and the dolphin begins learning to substitute somebody's hand for the target. The height that the dolphin finally rises out of the water depends on its strength and size. One rose nine feet, and the trainer had to stand on a stool to shake hands!

The most exciting way to experience the special bond between dolphins and people is to rub noses with them in the water. At first it is a little scary. The dolphins are enormous, and they zoom past visitors and up to them at great speeds, spraying water everywhere. Then, as the trainer instructs them, the visitors place their arms out to the side, slap the water lightly, and wait. A few seconds later, one or two dolphins glide up to them from behind and place their dorsal fins in the visitors' hands. When the visitors grab on, the dolphins take off! It is a fast spin, with water splashing all around, until the dolphins reach the dock, when they dive, letting the visitors know that the game is over.

The dolphins are affectionate with people, but only when they want to be. Sometimes they are so interested that a visitor walking on the dock might notice one swimming alongside, cocking its head, studying the visitor with one big brown eye. Sometimes the dolphins are not at all engaged by playing, and then, no matter what the visitors do, they won't go near the dock. But at the right moment, a visitor can sit on the dock, splash his hand lightly, and a dolphin will go over and put its snout in the hand to be petted. Or if the visitor taps his own shoulder, the dolphin may lift its snout right up on the visitor's shoulder in a hug. A few of the dolphins will even collect seaweed gifts from the sea bottom and present them to a visitor in exchange for a free fish.

Babies are born frequently at the Dolphin Research Center. Because dolphins are mammals, the babies emerge directly from their mothers rather than from eggs, and they are fed their mothers' milk for about a year and a half to two years. Dolphins are pregnant for twelve months and generally deliver only one baby per pregnancy. Twins *have* been born to dolphins, but they have never survived, because the mothers cannot take care of more than one active baby at a time.

When dolphin babies are born, they are almost one-third the size of their mothers. In order to breathe, they must swim to the surface immediately, so if necessary the mothers push them up. They stay close to their mothers for at least a year, always swimming with them, with the baby shadowing the mother's movements. Whenever there is a birth at the center, the staff celebrates as if the baby were one of their own.

Sick animals sent to the Dolphin Research Center are usually healed. Living in the relaxed natural environment among people who are charmed by them seems to help immeasurably. Dolphins sometimes suffer in aquariums because they have no privacy, are not living in natural seawater surroundings, and are disturbed by seeing their reflections in the glass tanks. Dolphins are so sensitive that they get the same illnesses people get when they are upset. When his trainer went away, one dolphin was so lonely that he stopped eating. But he cheered up on hearing the familiar whistles and commands, and ate his best meal in weeks.

Working with sick dolphins is difficult. When these huge animals are removed from the water for treatment, they suffer great stress. And they cannot have surgery successfully, because they stop breathing under anesthesia.

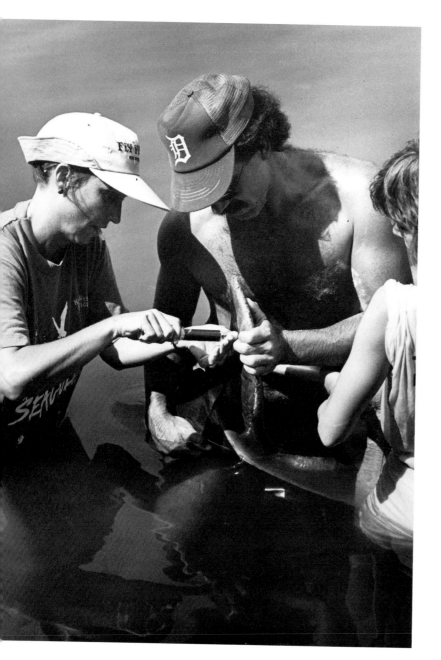

Nai-Aili came to the Dolphin Research Center in 1982, when he was discovered lying on the beach next door, badly malnourished. He weighed only one hundred fifty pounds, when he should have weighed at least five hundred. Everyone thought he would die, but they gave him constant care until he was able to stay afloat and eat on his own. Nai was not a bottlenose dolphin like all the others. He was an offshore dolphin, the only one of his kind in captivity at the time.

At first the other dolphins wouldn't have anything to do with Nai, perhaps because he was used to sending out signals in deeper water and therefore couldn't communicate with them. But eventually they all became friends.

Then, in 1987, Nai became ill again, with liver problems. He weighed only four hundred pounds and was quite sunburned from lying on the surface too much instead of swimming. Several times a week, Mandy, Jayne, and the staff put Nai on a stretcher, rubbed white sunburn medicine all over his body, injected B vitamins into him, and took some blood for testing. Mandy and Jayne, who are capable of performing any routine medical procedure, frequently called in veterinarians. Sadly, though, Nai was not able to recover and died a few months later.

But around the same time, another dolphin—who was given the name Dart—was found floating off southern Florida by some fishermen. Mandy and the staff went to pick her up and bring her back to the center. Dart was starving and dehydrated, and the staff believed she had been separated from her family of dolphins and wouldn't have survived long alone.

Also an offshore dolphin, Dart, too, was different from the Atlantic bottlenoses at the center. Because she was so different—and small, only four feet long—Mandy and Jayne kept her separated from the others. They were afraid she would be injured by them. At first Dart got better, but then she became sluggish and stopped eating. As her health got worse and worse, they suspected that it was because she had no contact with the other dolphins. Finally Mandy tried an experiment that he hoped would save her life. He put Dart into the pool with Bee, who was pregnant. He held on to Dart until Bee started circling with curiosity. After a long time, he let Dart go, and eventually Bee was at ease enough to carry Dart along in her wake to the main pool. Now Dart is one of the gang and is especially close to Omega, Bee's baby.

An important new project at the Dolphin Research Center is training two dolphins, Joe and Rosie, to be released into the open sea. They were found nine years ago and have lived in captivity ever since. If they were released now, they would not be able to survive, because they do not know how to catch or eat live fish.

How does the trainer teach them these essential skills? First he throws "chum," ground-up frozen fish, into the pen where they live. This attracts live fish such as snapper and mullet into the area. The trainer hooks them and cuts off the tails so that Rosie and Joe can catch the slow-moving fish. It may take several months for them to learn how to do this.

But it is not enough for the dolphins to be able to catch fish. They must also be able to live without human beings, after being so involved with them. Often the freed dolphins swim up on the beach, looking for human contact.

Joe and Rosie have been given identifying marks on their dorsal fins. These marks will be printed on a poster with a phone number that people are to call if they spot the dolphins in the ocean. When they are ready, Joe and Rosie will be flown to the ocean off Georgia, where there are few fishermen and predators, a lot of food, and many other dolphins. There they will be put in temporary pens while they adjust to the change. Then the pens will be opened, and Joe and Rosie will have the choice of staying in them and being returned to the center—or going free. Which, we wonder, will they choose?

The Dolphin Research Center is always striving to know dolphins better and to help every human reach these amazing creatures. The goal is to *really* penetrate their world and to communicate with dolphins as we never have with any other creature. Perhaps when we solve the mystery of these gentle giants, we will understand not only dolphins—but ourselves, as well.